D1712270

MIGHTY MACHINES

Road Rollers

by Derek Zobel

BELLWETHER MEDIA • MINNEAPOLIS, MN

Note to Librarians, Teachers, and Parents:

Blastoff! Readers are carefully developed by literacy experts and combine standards-based content with developmentally appropriate text.

Level 1 provides the most support through repetition of high-frequency words, light text, predictable sentence patterns, and strong visual support.

Level 2 offers early readers a bit more challenge through varied simple sentences, increased text load, and less repetition of high-frequency words.

Level 3 advances early-fluent readers toward fluency through increased text and concept load, less reliance on visuals, longer sentences, and more literary language.

Level 4 builds reading stamina by providing more text per page, increased use of punctuation, greater variation in sentence patterns, and increasingly challenging vocabulary.

Level 5 encourages children to move from "learning to read" to "reading to learn" by providing even more text, varied writing styles, and less familiar topics.

Whichever book is right for your reader, Blastoff! Readers are the perfect books to build confidence and encourage a love of reading that will last a lifetime!

This edition first published in 2010 by Bellwether Media, Inc.

No part of this publication may be reproduced in whole or in part without written permission of the publisher. For information regarding permission, write to Bellwether Media, Inc., Attention: Permissions Department, Post Office Box 19349, Minneapolis, MN 55419.

Library of Congress Cataloging-in-Publication Data
Zobel, Derek, 1983–
 Road rollers / by Derek Zobel.
  p. cm. – (Blastoff! readers. Mighty machines)
 Includes bibliographical references and index.
 Summary: "Simple text and full color photographs introduce beginning readers to road rollers. Developed by literary experts for students in kindergarten through grade 3"–Provided by publisher.
 ISBN 978-1-60014-266-6 (hardcover : alk. paper)
 1. Road rollers–Juvenile literature. I. Title.

TE223.Z63 2010
625.8–dc22

2009008277

Contents

What Are Road Rollers?	4
Road Roller Drums	8
Road Rollers at Work	16
Glossary	22
To Learn More	23
Index	24

Road rollers are heavy machines. They use their **weight** to flatten ground.

Road rollers
flatten ground
for roads and
buildings.

A road roller has a **drum**. Drums are smooth or rough.

drum

Rough drums work well on dirt and rock. This road roller has one rough drum and two wheels.

This road roller has two rough drums. It flattens trash in a **landfill**.

Smooth drums are used on **asphalt**. This road roller has two smooth drums.

This road roller flattens ground for a **foundation**. A building will be built on it.

This road
roller flattens
asphalt to
make a road.

Now cars can
drive on the
new road!

Glossary

asphalt—a mix of crushed rock and other materials used to pave roads

drum—a part of a machine shaped like a tube with ends; road rollers use drums to flatten ground.

foundation—a solid, flat structure on which a building is built

landfill—a large area where trash is buried

weight—how heavy a person or object is

To Learn More

AT THE LIBRARY

Randolph, Joanne. *Road Rollers*. New York, N.Y.: Rosen, 2002.

Raynor, Derek A. *Road Rollers*. Oxford, England: Shire Library, 2008.

Zemlicka, Shannon. *From Rock to Road*. Minneapolis, Minn.: Lerner, 2004.

ON THE WEB

Learning more about mighty machines is as easy as 1, 2, 3.

1. Go to www.factsurfer.com.

2. Enter "mighty machines" into the search box.

3. Click the "Surf" button and you will see a list of related Web sites.

With factsurfer.com, finding more information is just a click away.

Index

asphalt, 14, 18

buildings, 6, 16

cars, 20

dirt, 10

drum, 8, 10, 12, 14

foundation, 16

ground, 4, 6, 16

landfill, 12

roads, 6, 18, 20

rock, 10

trash, 12

weight, 4

wheels, 10

The images in this book are reproduced through the courtesy of: Andre Günther, front cover, p. 21; Dbvirago, p. 5; Agg, p. 7; Dennis McDonald, p. 9; Rafal Olechowski, p. 11; David R. Frazier Photolibrary, Inc., p. 13; Filip Fuxa, p. 15; Andre Comeau, p. 17; Caterpillar Inc., p. 19.